Lent–A Season to Sit in the Ashes

We begin the season of Lent with ashes on our foreheads. What is symbolised by this smudging? Perhaps the heart understands better than the head because more people go to church on Ash Wednesday than on any other day of the year, including Christmas. Why are the ashes so popular?

Their popularity, I suspect, comes from the fact that, as a symbol, they are blunt, archetypal and speak the language of the soul. Something inside each of us knows exactly why we take the ashes: "Dust thou art and into dust thou shalt return!" No doctor of metaphysics need explain this.

To put on ashes, to sit in ashes, is to say publicly and to yourself that you are reflective, in a penitential mode, that this is not "ordinary time" for you, that you are grieving some of the things you have done

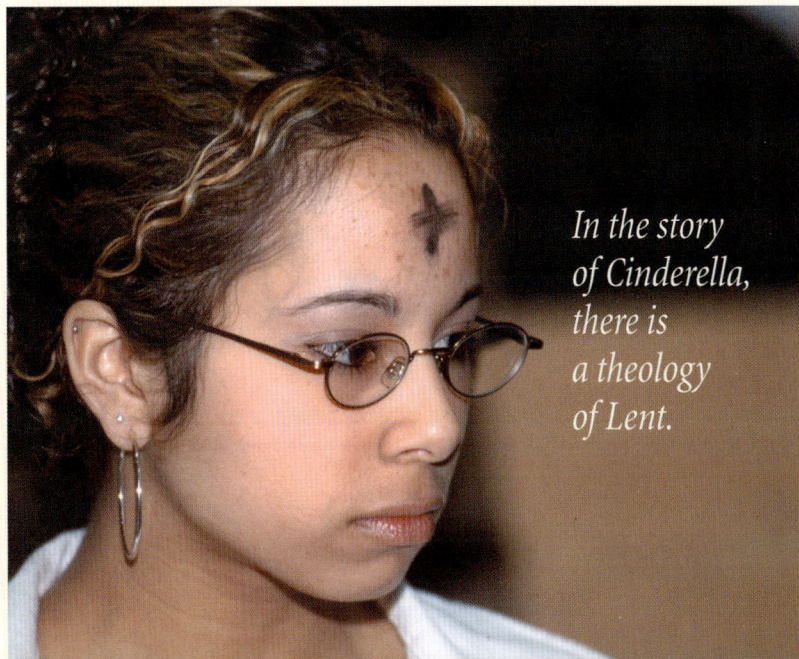

In the story of Cinderella, there is a theology of Lent.

3

or lost, that some important work is going on silently inside you. You are, metaphorically and really, in the cinders of a dead fire, waiting for a fuller day in your life.

All of this has deep roots. There is something innate to the human soul that knows that, every so often, one must make a journey of descent, be smudged, lose one's lustre, and wait while the ashes do their work. All ancient traditions abound with stories of having to sit in the ashes before one can be transformed.

We all know, for example, the story of Cinderella. This is a centuries-old wisdom-tale that speaks about the value of ashes. The name, Cinderella, itself already says most of it. Literally it means: "the young girl who sits in the cinders". Moreover, as the tale makes plain, before the glass slipper is placed on her foot, before the beautiful gown, ball, dance, and marriage, there must first be a period of being humbled. In the story of Cinderella, there is a theology of Lent.

The Church taps into this deep well of wisdom when it puts ashes on our foreheads at the beginning of Lent. Lent is a season for each of us to sit in the ashes, waiting while some silent growth takes place within us, and simply being still so that the ashes can do their work in us.

The Desert as a Place

"Every tear brings the refrain in Jewish apocalyptic literature and expressed the belief that a certain quota of tears had first to be shed before any true joy could inhabit us. They understood this mystically, not literally. In order to be filled by God one must first be emptied.

The desert does this for you. It empties you. It is not a place where you can decide how you want to grow and change. But it is an experience that you undergo, expose yourself to and have the courage to face. The idea is not so much that you do things there, but that things happen to you while there – silent, unseen, transforming things. The desert purifies you, almost against your will, through God's efforts.

In the desert, what really occurs is a cosmic confrontation between God and the devil; though this happens within and through you. Your job is only to have the courage to be there. The idea is that God does the work, providing you have the courage to show up.

In terms of an image, this is what Lent is meant to be, time in the desert to courageously face the chaos and the demons within us and to let God do battle with them through us. The result is that we are purified, made ready, so the intoxicating joy of Easter might then bind us more closely to God and each other.

*In order to be filled by God
one must first be emptied.*

Facing Our Demons in the Desert

We live lives of tortured complexity. Inside each of us there is both a saint and a sinner and enough complexity to write our own book on abnormal psychology. Our hearts are a murky cauldron of grace and sin, angels and demons. Always, it seems, we are torn in a way that leaves us feeling unsure, guilty, and tense.

To go into the desert means to stare our inner chaos in the face. What demons live inside this chaos? The demons of the prodigal son, grandiosity and unbridled sexuality; and the demons of his older brother, paranoia and joylessness.

Grandiosity is the demon that tells us that we are the centre of the universe, that our lives are more important than those of others. Unbridled sexuality is the demon of obsession, addiction, and lust. Its urge is to bracket everything else – sacred commitment, moral ideal, and personal consequences – for a single, furtive pleasure.

Paranoia is the demon of bitterness, anger, and jealousy. It makes us believe that life has cheated us, that the celebration is always about others and never about us. This demon fills us with the urge to be cynical, cold, distrustful, and cursing. Finally, the last demon in this family tells us that joylessness is maturity, that cynicism is wisdom, and that bitterness is justice. This is the demon that keeps us from entering the room of celebration and joining the dance.

All of these demons are inside every one of us. To stare them in the face is to enter the desert. A scary thing? Yes, but the Scriptures assure us that if we muster the courage to face them, God will send angels to minister to us.

*To go into the desert means
to stare our inner chaos in the face.*

6

Acknowledge Your Own Complexity

I once saw an interview with Catherine de Hueck Doherty, a Russian baroness and the founder of the Madonna House Apostolate. She was already more than 80 years old and, reflecting on the struggles of her spiritual journey, said something to this effect:

"It's like there are three persons inside me. There's someone I call the baroness. The baroness is spiritual and given over to asceticism and prayer. She's the one who founded the religious community, wrote the spiritual books, and who tries to give her life to the poor. But inside of me too there's another person whom I call Catherine. Catherine likes idleness, long baths, fine clothes, putting on make-up, good meals, good wine, and as a married woman enjoyed a healthy sex life. She doesn't want renunciation or poverty. She's not religious like the baroness. Indeed, she hates the baroness and has a strained relationship with her.

"And, finally, inside of me too, there's someone else, a little girl, a child lying on a hillside in Finland, watching the clouds and daydreaming. And, as I get older, I feel more like the baroness, long more for Catherine, but think that maybe the little girl daydreaming on a hillside in Finland might be who I really am."

These words come from a spiritual giant, someone who attained both wholeness and sanctity after a long search and difficult struggle. Like Catherine Doherty, all of us have a number of different persons inside us. Wholeness means somehow making a whole, a harmony, out of all these different persons.

*All of us have a number
of different persons inside us.*

Listening to Christ's Heartbeat

The Last Supper account in John's Gospel contains a curious picture. The evangelist describes the beloved disciple as reclining on the breast of Jesus. What is contained in his image? A picture of how each of us should be focused as we look out at the world.

When you put your head upon the breast of another, your ear is just above that person's heart and you are able to hear his or her heartbeat. Thus, in John's image, we see the beloved disciple with his ear on Jesus' heart and his eyes peering out at the world.

This is an image, a mystical one. Among other things, it is a picture of gentleness. What it shows, however, is not a saccharine piety, a sweetness hard to swallow, but a softness that comes from being at peace, from being so rooted and centred in a love that one can look out at the world without bitterness, anger, jealousy, the sense of being cheated, and the need to blame or compete with others.

In John's Gospel, it is also a eucharistic image. What we see there, the image of a person with his ear on Jesus' heart, is how John wants us to imagine ourselves when we are at Eucharist. In its reality, that is what the Eucharist is, a physical reclining on the breast of Jesus. It is also an image of how we should touch God and be sustained by him in solitude.

CORBIS

Touching Our Solitude

Henri Nouwen once said: "By touching the centre of our solitude, we sense that we have been touched by loving hands."

Deep inside each of us, like a brand, there is a place where God has touched, caressed, and kissed us. Long before memory, long before we ever remember touching or loving or kissing anyone or anything, or being touched by anything or anybody in this world, there is a different kind of memory, the memory of being gently touched by loving hands.

There is an ancient legend which holds that when an infant is created God kisses its soul and sings to it. As its guardian angel carries it to earth to join its body, she also sings to it. The legend says that God's kiss and his song, as well as the song of the angel, remain in that soul for ever – to be called up, cherished, shared, and to become the basis of all of our songs.

But to feel that kiss, to hear that song, requires solitude. I do not feel gentleness when inside of me and all around me there is noise, abrasiveness, anger, bitterness, jealousy, competitiveness, and paranoia. The sound of God's heartbeat is audible only in solitude and in the gentleness it brings.

An ancient legend holds that
when an infant is created
God kisses its soul and sings to it.

The Desert, a Womb of Emptiness

The idea of the desert has played a prominent part in the spirituality of all religions. The desert is the place where we feel our smallness; where, stripped of all that normally buoys us up, we feel how lonely, helpless, fragile, and mortal we really are.

Great religious persons have always understood this and that is why so many of them, Jesus included, often went physically into some desert to place themselves into a womb of emptiness. This kind of desert, as we know, is not just a physical, geographical thing. It is also a place in the soul. More particularly, it is that place in the soul where we feel most alone, insubstantial, and frightened.

This feeling of loneliness brings with it too a sense of helplessness and dependence. In the desert, alone among the barren sands, painful realisations break through: "Everything I rely on can easily disappear. It's fragile. I'm fragile. I could disappear."

We have no real maturity until our souls are shaped by that realisation. The desert, letting emptiness work in us, is what re-gestates the soul. Emptiness is a womb. It remoulds the soul and lets us be born again, adults still, but now aware. Aware as we once were as small children, that there can be no life and meaning outside of acknowledging our littleness and reaching out, as do infants, to a great providence and a great love outside of us.

Emptiness is a womb.
It remoulds the soul and
lets us be born again.

In the Desert, God Is Close to Us

In her biography, *The Long Loneliness*, Dorothy Day shares how, shortly after her conversion to Catholicism, she went through a painful, desert time. Her prayer at the time was wrenching, naked. She describes how she laid bare her helplessness, spilling out her confusion, her doubts, her fears, and her temptations to bitterness and despair. In essence, she said to God: "I have given up everything that ever supported me, in trust, to you. I have nothing left. You need to do something for me, soon. I can't keep this up much longer."

She was, biblically speaking, in the desert – alone, without support, helpless before a chaos that threatened to overwhelm her – and, as was the case with Jesus, both in the desert and in Gethsemane, God "sent angels to minister to her". God steadied her in the chaos. She returned to New York and, that night, as she walked up to her apartment she saw a man sitting there. His name was Peter Maurin. Together they started the *Catholic Worker*.

We should not be surprised that her prayer had such a tangible result. The desert, Scripture assures us, is the place where God is especially near. In the desert we are exposed, made vulnerable to be overwhelmed by chaos and temptations of every kind. But, because we are so stripped of everything we normally rely on, this is also a privileged moment for grace. Why? Because when we are helpless we are open. That is why the desert is both the place of chaos and the place of God's closeness.

The desert is both the place of chaos
and the place of God's closeness.

The Restless Spirit

Almost everything within our world inhibits our journey inward towards stillness and silence. Our culture invites excitement, not silence; activity, not stillness. Thus we find ourselves constantly titillated and overstimulated in our restlessness. Somehow the impression is out there that everyone in the whole world is finding something that you are not, that everyone's life is more full and complete than yours, that your life, as it is, is too small and timid, and that only if you bring many more people, things, places, and experiences into your life will you find peace and calm.

The world suggests that the solution to your restlessness lies outside of yourself, in building a bigger and more exciting life. If you are lonely, find a friend; if you are restless, do something; if you have a desire, fulfil it. It trivialises our restlessness, inviting us in a thousand ways to forget that God has called us to make an inward pilgrimage.

In the preface to Elizabeth O'Connor's book, *Search for Silence*, N. Gordon Cosby writes, "The one journey that ultimately matters is the journey into the place of stillness deep within one's self. To reach that place is to be home; to fail to reach it is to be forever restless." This challenge should be written in bold letters in the preface of every spiritual book today. Too much inside of us and around us invites us to forget this and it is too dangerous to forget it. It's our rest, our peace, that's at stake here.

The one journey that ultimately matters is the journey into the place of stillness deep within one's self.

Cultivating Loneliness

Few persons in recent centuries have touched the human heart as deeply as has Søren Kierkegaard, the Danish philosopher. There are many reasons for this, some of which are obvious. He was a man of rare brilliance, with a lot to give others. One of the reasons that he was able to so deeply and exceptionally touch people's hearts, however, had less to do with his brilliance than it had to with his suffering, especially his loneliness.

As a young man, he fell deeply in love and, for a time, planned marriage with the woman to whom he was passionately attached. However, at one stage, at great emotional cost to himself and (so history would suggest) at even greater emotional cost to the woman involved, he broke off the engagement and set himself to live for the rest of his life as a celibate.

His reasoning was simple. He felt that what he had to give to the world came more from his own loneliness. He could share deeply because, first of all, he felt deeply. Loneliness gave him depth. Rightly or wrongly, he judged that marriage might in some way deflect or distract him from that depth, painful as it was.

Albert Camus once suggested that it is in solitude and loneliness that we find the threads that bind human community. Kierkegaard understood this and he embraced it to the point that he positively cultivated his own loneliness. In loneliness and longing, empathy is born. When nothing is foreign to us nobody will be foreign to us – and our words will begin to heal others.

In loneliness and longing,
empathy is born.

The Unfinished Symphony

"In the event of the insufficiency of everything attainable, we come to understand that here, in this life, all symphonies remain unfinished." Karl Rahner wrote those words and not to understand them is to risk letting restlessness become a cancer in our lives.

We are congenitally over-charged and over-built for this earth, infinite spirits living in a finite situation, hearts made for union with everything and everybody meeting only mortal persons and things. Small wonder we have problems with insatiability, daydreams, loneliness, and restlessness. We are Grand Canyons without a bottom. Nothing, short of union with all that is, can ever fill in that void. To be tormented by restlessness is to be human.

But in truly accepting that humanity we become a bit more easeful in our restlessness. As Rahner puts it, in this life there is no finished symphony, everything comes with an undertow of restlessness and inadequacy. This is true of everyone.

Peace and restfulness can come to us only when we accept that fact because it is only then that we will stop demanding that life – our spouses, our families, our friends, our jobs, our vocations, and vacations – give us something that they cannot give, namely, the finished symphony, clear-cut pure joy, complete consummation.

*We are Grand Canyons
without a bottom.*

Offer Up Your Priestly Prayers

One of the responsibilities of being an adult is that of praying for the world, like the high priests of old. Indeed, we are all priests, ordained by the oils of baptism and consecrated by the burdens of life that have given us wrinkles and grey hair. All of us, lay and cleric alike, need to offer up priestly prayer each day.

How do we pray priestly prayer? By praying the prayer of the Church, namely, the Eucharist. This kind of prayer, called liturgy, is what keeps incarnate the priestly prayer of Christ. In essence, we are saying: "Lord, God, I stand before you as a microcosm of the earth itself. See in my openness, the world's openness; in my infidelity, the world's infidelity; in my generosity, the world's generosity; in my selfishness, the world's selfishness; in my desire to praise you, the world's desire to praise you. For I am of the earth, a piece of earth, and the earth opens or closes to you through my body, my soul, and my voice. I am your priest on earth, and what I hold up for you today is all that is in this world, both of joy and of suffering."

To pray like this is to pray liturgically, as a priest. We take on a universal voice offering prayers and entreaties, aloud and in silent tears, to God for the sake of the world.

W.P. WITTMAN

Facing in a New Direction

"Repent and believe in the good news!" These are the first words out of Jesus' mouth in Mark's Gospel and they are meant as a summary of the entire gospel. But what do these words mean? In English, the word "repent" is often misunderstood. It seems to imply that we have already done something wrong, regret it and now commit ourselves to live in a new way. Repentance, understood in this way, means to live beyond a sinful past. Biblically, this is not quite what is meant.

In the gospels, the particular word used for repentance is *metanoia*. This means to do an about-face, to turn around, to face in an entirely new direction. It takes its root in two Greek words: *meta* – beyond; and *nous* – mind. Literally, *metanoia* means to move beyond our present mindset, beyond our present way of seeing things.

It is interesting to consider that many of the miracles of Jesus are connected to opening up or otherwise healing someone's eyes, ears, or tongue. Eyes are opened in order to see more deeply and spiritually; ears are opened in order to hear things more compassionately; and tongues are loosened in order to praise God more freely and to speak words of reconciliation and love to each other. To repent is to allow God to open our minds and heal us so that indeed we can turn and face in a completely new direction.

------

*To repent is to allow God
to open our minds and heal us.*

Virtue in Self-sacrifice

Previous generations had a certain sense of sacrifice which, for better and for worse, we have all but lost. In my parents' generation, to offer just one kind of example, it was not that uncommon for someone in a family to forgo his or her own private ambitions in order to stay at home and take care of an ageing or sick parent. For years that person would put his or her own life on hold while essentially he or she lived for someone else. Very often, by the time the parent died, it was too late for that person to build the kind of life that might have been possible – marriage, children, a career – had not circumstances conscripted him or her to do this family duty.

Today we no longer see virtue in that kind of self-sacrifice. On the contrary, we tend to frown upon it and judge it negatively, as a failure of nerve, a tragedy, the waste of a life! Irrespective of whether that is true, previous generations did recognise something that today we often don't perceive, namely, that in this life we are essentially interdependent. We have duties as well as rights. Moreover, this kind of sacrifice is, in the end, the cornerstone of family and community life. Might not the cause of some of our current difficulties in keeping our marriages, families, and communities together be the breakdown of this kind of self-sacrifice?

*In this life we are
essentially interdependent.
We have duties as well as rights.*

A Service That Is Sure

There is a story about St Christopher, probably more legend than truth, which runs this way: As a youth, Christopher was gifted in every way, except faith. He was physically strong, good-hearted, mellow, and well liked by all. He was also generous, using his physical strength to help others. His one fault was that he found it hard to believe in God. This, however, did not prevent him from using his gifts to serve others. He became a ferry-boat operator, spending his life helping to carry people across a dangerous river. One night, during a storm, the ferry-boat capsized and Christopher dived into the dark waters to rescue a young child. Carrying that child to the shore, he gazed upon the child and saw there the face of Christ.

The story gives us an answer, a practical one, to one of the most difficult questions of all: What should we do when our faith is weak? Christopher's answer: Use your gifts to help others. God does not ask us to have a faith that is certain, but a service that is sure. God, the author and source of all reality, is neither angered nor threatened by an honest agnosticism. There are, for every one of us, dark nights of the soul, silences of God, cold lonely seasons, bitter times when God's appearances to us cannot be truly grasped or recognised. But if we faithfully help carry others, we will one day find ourselves before the person of Christ.

---

*God does not ask us
to have a faith that is certain,
but a service that is sure.*

The Line Between Victims and Saints

When is one a victim and when is one giving one's life for others? At the level of outward appearance, this can be indistinguishable. Outward action is not the criterion, inward freedom is. I am a victim when somebody takes my life. I am practising selfless virtue when I freely give it.

Jesus illustrates this. As he sacrifices freely his life, renouncing consistently his own needs in the face of the needs of others, he keeps repeating, as if a mantra: "Nobody takes my life from me. I give it freely."

It is from this, Jesus' example of a love that freely sacrifices unto death, that we must learn. Nobody escapes the unfairness of life and nobody, other than a complete monster, goes through life without ever putting other people's needs ahead of his or her own. The challenge of the gospel is to move from bitter victim to joyful giver.

Jesus was not a bitter victim, he made that plain in the Garden of Gethsemane and again before Pilate. He chose to lay down his life. It was a free decision, made in love. Nobody can take by force what one gives for free.

The challenge of the gospel is
to move from bitter victim
to joyful giver.

Face to Face With Our Inadequacy

Some 20 years ago, while on retreat, an elderly nun was assigned to me as director. She proved to be a woman of rare maturity, providing the guidance that I needed at the time. Being young and intense, I too easily made a cosmic drama and tragedy out of every ordinary desolation or setback. She challenged me with a wisdom, an earthiness, and a sense of humour that continually helped deflate my pompousness. At one stage of the retreat, sensing my Hamlet-type propensities, she gave me a little proverb: Fear not, you are inadequate!

Through the years, that little adage has come back to me, off and on, mostly at times when I have been a bit overwhelmed. There is a certain consolation in it. Whether you are a parent, a teacher, a minister, a priest, an advocate for justice, or simply a friend to someone in need, there are countless times when you come face to face with your own inadequacy. It is healthy, humbling, and uplifting to accept the fact that we are not God and that we are not asked to try to be.

Fear not, you are inadequate! To accept the truth of that proverb is to make a little prayer.

Fear not, you are inadequate!

Waiting for a Fuller Season

Henri Nouwen used to say that 98 per cent of our lives is spent in waiting. At a superficial level, we experience this in the amount of time we spend waiting at checkout counters, in airports, for buses, for somebody to arrive, or for something to end – our workday, a class, a church service, a bout of the flu. But that is the superficial part of it.

More important is the fact that almost all the time we are waiting for a fuller season for our lives. Rarely do we have what Nouwen calls "a fully pregnant moment", namely, a moment when we can say to ourselves: "Right now, I don't want to be any other place, with any other persons, or doing anything else than what I am doing right now!"

Isn't it rather stoic and joy-killing to accept that life is 98 per cent about waiting? On the contrary, to accept this is not masochistic, but freeing. My parents' generation did this by saying, each day, the prayer: "For now we live, mourning and weeping in this valley of tears." Praying like this didn't turn them into cold stoics. Instead, knowing that the fuller season for which we wait cannot be found here, they were able to enjoy, perhaps more so than can our own generation, the simple joys that are possible.

---

*Almost all the time
we are waiting for a
fuller season in our lives.*

The Real Presence

Once upon a time there was a rabbi. Whenever he wanted God's presence, he went to a special place in the woods, lit a fire, said some prayers, and did a dance. Then God would appear to him. When the rabbi died, his disciple did the same. If he wanted God's presence, he went to the same spot in the woods, lit the fire, and said the same prayers. Nobody had taught him the dance, but it still worked. God appeared. The next disciple carried on the tradition. Although he didn't know the prayers, nor the dance, he went to the same spot in the woods and lit the fire. God came.

Eventually a disciple came along who didn't know how to light the fire or say the prayers or do the dance. He searched for the place in the woods, but couldn't find it. All he knew was how to tell the story. But it worked. He discovered that whenever he told the story of how the others had found God, God would appear.

Ritual is best understood through metaphor, through story, as with the tale just told. God appears whenever certain stories get told. When we ritually tell the story of Jesus' sacrifice (in the Eucharistic Prayer, the very heart of liturgy) we experience the "real presence" of the event of Christ's dying and rising. Moreover, that reality is given to us so that we might participate in it. We, the congregation, die to the things that divide us and become the body and blood of Christ.

GENE PLAISTED, OSC

Therapy of Public Life

While doing my doctoral studies in Belgium, I was privileged to be able to attend the lectures of Antoine Vergote, a renowned doctor of both psychology and the soul. I asked him one day how one should handle emotional obsessions, both within oneself and when trying to help others. His answer surprised me. He said something to this effect: "God and prayer can and do help. But obsessional problems are mainly problems of over-concentration... and over-concentration is broken mainly by getting outside of yourself, outside of your own mind and heart and room. Get involved in public things – from entertainment, to politics, to work. Get outside of your closed world!"

Monks, with their monastic rhythm, have long understood this: Programme, rhythm, public participation, the demand to show up, the discipline of the monastic bell has kept many a man and woman sane – and relatively happy besides.

More specifically for us Christians: the therapy of public life means the therapy of an ecclesial life. We become emotionally well, steadier, less obsessed, less a slave of our own restlessness, by participating fully and healthily within the public life of the Church. Regular Eucharist, regular prayer with others, regular meetings to share faith, and regular duties and responsibilities within ministry not only nurture our spiritual lives, they also keep us sane and steady.

The monastic bell has kept many a man and woman sane.

The Original Sin

The story of the fall of Adam and Eve is coloured throughout, especially at the end (nakedness and shame), with sexual imagery, so much so that we can easily conclude that their transgression was of a sexual nature. It wasn't. The sexual motif in the story is a metaphor, an image of rape. Adam and Eve took, as by force, something that can only be received in love.

The condition that God gave Adam and Eve might be summarised this way: "I am giving you life. I will bathe you in life. But you must receive it and never take it. As long as you receive it, it will always be life-giving. But on the day you begin to take, rather than receive, your actions will begin to deal death, distrust, alienation, nakedness, and shame." That single commandment encapsulates all morality. It's the same with love. Something is only love, and it can only give life, when it is freely given. This condition is part of love's DNA.

The original sin of Adam and Eve wasn't sexual, but it was an act of rape. They wrongfully took what was intended as gift. Our culture, which rewards aggressiveness and tells us that we are foolish not to take for ourselves the good things we want, too often invites us to do the same thing.

Something is only love,
and it can only give life,
when it is freely given.

All We Have to Do Is Surrender

The gospel is not as much about worthiness as it is about surrender. What God wants from us is not a million acts of virtue, but a million acts of surrender, culminating in one massive surrender of soul, mind, and body. When we have given up everything and are completely helpless to give ourselves anything, as we will all eventually be when we face death, then salvation can be given to us.

And that is the key, salvation can only be given. It can never be taken, earned or possessed by right. Nothing we have or can accumulate in this life – fame, fortune, health, good looks, a good name, or even moral virtue, religious fidelity, personal sanctity, or the practice of social justice – tips God's hand towards us. What tips God's hand is helplessness, surrender in grace.

In the ideal order of things, surrender is for the mature. That is less true of us during the first half of our lives, for we are still building, but it becomes the deepest truth of the second half of life. After 40, understood religiously, life is not about claiming worthiness, or about building things, especially our own egos, but about getting in touch with helplessness.

Age brings us physically to our knees and more and more everything we have so painstakingly built up begins to mean less and less. That is the order of things. Salvation is not about great achievements, but about a great embrace. All we have to do is surrender.

Salvation is not about
great achievements,
but about a great embrace.

The Principle of Blessing

No one can truly bless another without dying. That's what makes a blessing so powerful. Nature prescribes that. Imagine a flower: As a seedling and budding young flower it is essentially selfish, consumed with its own growth. That remains true until it reaches the stage just past its bloom. At that point, it begins to die and in that movement it gives off its seed and is then consumed with giving itself away.

There are myriad lessons in that about mature love, mature sexuality, and mature growth. In the movement from seedling to young plant to bloom to giving off seed in death, we see nature's paradigm for maturity and generativity. In a flower, when full maturity is reached, life becomes consumed in giving itself away at the cost of its own death.

You see this in blessing adults – good mothers, fathers, teachers, clergy, mentors, uncles, aunts, and friends of all kinds. These, the generative adults, do not look like Peter Pan or Tinkerbell (who look like children), nor do they look like movie stars or professional athletes. No. Blessing adults, of both genders, are recognised by their stretch marks, their scars, their physical waning, and by the very fact that they are dying. They are not obsessed with preserving their bloom.

That is nature's lesson. Generativity depends upon a willingness to die and to let go of our seed so that the other can bloom.

---

*Generativity depends upon
a willingness to die and
to let go of our seed.*

Dying to Give Life

If I want to really bless someone, I must, in some way, give my life to that person so as to enable him or her to have more life. We see this aspect of blessing powerfully portrayed in Victor Hugo's classic novel, *Les Misérables*. At one point in that story, Jean Valjean, who is by then an old man, goes in search of Marius, the young man who is in love with his adopted daughter. Initially his motivation for searching out Marius is mixed. He is understandably threatened by this young man who will take his daughter away from him. He finds Marius with a group of idealistic young revolutionaries who, while trying to help the poor, have put themselves into a position where they are all about to be killed in a brutal attack from government forces. Their position is hopeless.

It is in this situation that Jean Valjean finds young Marius asleep. He bends over him, invokes God ("God on high, hear my prayer") then, turning to young Marius, he repeats several times: "Look on this boy… he is young, he's afraid… tomorrow he might die but, Lord, let him live – let me die, let him live! Let him live!"

Those last lines are the prototype of deep blessing. A deep blessing is not simply an affirmation: "You are a fine young man!" "You are a gifted young woman!" Good and life-giving as these words are, they are not enough. To bless someone deeply is to die for them in some real way, to give up some part of your life for them.

*To bless someone deeply
is to die for them
in some real way.*

A Paschal Prescription

There is an old adage, now the motto for Outward Bound programmes in the USA, that reads, "If you can't get out of something, get more deeply into it." There is more than a little wisdom in that line, despite its rather glib sound. Taken seriously, it is a paschal prescription, a challenge to die so that we might live.

Christ illustrated what that means in his prayer in Gethsemane. First he prayed that he might get out of it: "Father, let this cup pass from me." Then, when he couldn't get out of it, he got deeply into it. The result was the Resurrection.

Many resurrections, for us, lie in imitating Christ in this. For example, today there are many people who are very unhappy with their churches but, for all kinds of reasons, can never leave those churches. If that is the case, then the prescription is clear: If you can't get out of it, get more deeply into it. Enter your church more deeply, see and experience in the tensions, pettiness, divisions, and angers of this particular community, the basic and universal struggle of all people to come together around one table, to have one heart.

The struggle for one community is, singularly, the most difficult and demanding of all human endeavours. Your local church offers you the laboratory to work at the project.

The struggle for one community is, singularly,
the most difficult and demanding
of all human endeavours.

The Secret to Prayer

We don't pray to make God present to us. God is always present everywhere. We pray to make ourselves present to God. God, as Sheila Cassidy colourfully puts it, is no more present in church than in a drinking bar, but we generally are more present to God in church than we are in a drinking bar. The problem of presence is not with God, but with us.

Sadly, this is also true for our presence to the richness of our own lives. Too often we are not present to the beauty, love, and grace that brim within the ordinary moments of our lives. Bounty is there, but we aren't. Because of restlessness, tiredness, obsession, haste, whatever, too often we are not enough inside of ourselves to appreciate what the moments of our own lives hold.

Viktor Frankl, the author of *Man's Search for Meaning*, was lucky. He was revived by doctors after being clinically dead for a few minutes. When he returned to his ordinary life, everything suddenly became very rich: "One very important aspect of post-mortem life is that everything gets precious, gets piercingly important. You get stabbed by things, by flowers and by babies and by beautiful things – just the very act of living, of walking and breathing and eating and having friends and chatting. One gets the much-intensified sense of miracles."

The secret to prayer is not to try to make God present, but to make ourselves present to God. The secret to finding beauty and love in life is the same. Like God, they are already present. The trick is to make ourselves present to them.

Anchored in the Rhythms of the Ordinary

Something inside us despises the ordinary. Something tells us that ordinary life, with its predictable routines, domestic rhythms, and conscription to duty makes for cheap meaning.

Inside us there is the sense that the ordinary can weigh us down and keep us from entering the more rewarding waters of passion, romance, and creativity. I remember a student of mine who shared in class that her greatest fear in life was to succumb to the ordinary, "to end up a content, little housewife and mother, happily doing laundry commercials!"

Life, Jesus assures us, is not meant to be lived in black and white, nor is it meant simply to be an endless cycle of rising, showering, going off to work, coming home, having supper, preparing for the next day, then going back to bed. And yet, there is much, much to be said for that seemingly small routine. The rhythm of the ordinary is, in the end, the deepest wellspring from which to draw joy and meaning.

Sometimes the mentor that teaches this is illness. When we regain our health and energy after having been ill and out of our normal routines, nothing is as sweet as returning to the ordinary – our work, our routine, the normal stuff of everyday life. Only after it has been taken away and then given back, do we realise that the clean simple appreciation of daily things is the ultimate treasure. There's a lot to be said for being a contented, little person, anchored in the rhythms of the ordinary.

Life, Jesus assures us, is not meant to be lived in black and white.

Of Suffering and Humiliation

I recently visited a friend dying of cancer. Her 50-year-old body, once remarkably beautiful, was grossly disfigured, wasted, smelled of death and, like the face of the suffering servant in Isaiah, was as much an object of revulsion as of attraction. A proud spirit, she lay humble, embarrassed, humiliated in her body. But God lay with her in that humiliation, shining forth, revealing secrets – revealing what was revealed on the cross.

Whenever we see someone who is unable to protect herself or himself against pain, especially the type of pain that humbles and humiliates, we are witnessing the humiliation of God in the world. And if we have the eyes of faith, we will know that we stand at that place where the deeper secrets of heaven are revealed.

We see it in an adult body ravaged by age, handicap, or terminal disease. We see this too whenever we see anyone who, for whatever reason, is perceived by others as naive, unattractive, stupid, or somehow an embarrassment to himself or herself.

To know God, one must begin to grasp the humiliation of God in this world. God shines brightly in our humiliations, unafraid to be embarrassed in this world.

To know God,
one must begin to grasp
the humiliation of God
in this world.

The Wounds of Christ

There is a story told, a legend perhaps, about St Teresa of Avila. One day the devil appeared to her, disguised as Christ. Teresa wasn't fooled for a second. She immediately dismissed him. But before he left, the devil asked her, "How did you know? How could you be so sure I wasn't Christ?" Her answer: "You didn't have any wounds! Christ has wounds."

Christ has wounds! So does anyone who stands where he stands. This is spiritual wisdom. To teach anything else is a sham.

Our culture quickly identifies lack of physical, emotional or social wholeness with lack of blessing. We identify Christ more with the unmarked body of youth (still taking more life than giving it) than with the stretch marks of life-giving adults. Thus, our real symbol for what constitutes life and blessing is the perfect body of an ever-younger Hollywood star, still unmarked by anything that might somehow humiliate it, rather than a stretched, misshapen body that has been scarred and made to sag by actually giving life. But the body of Christ is a humiliated body, permanently wounded by giving life.

When Jesus rose from the dead, the first thing he did was to show his disciples his wounds, glorified now, but extremely humiliating to him before he died. To become spiritually astute, as was Teresa of Avila, we must begin to understand what that means. Christ is ultimately recognised in his wounds.

When Jesus rose from the dead,
the first thing he did was
to show his disciples his wounds.

Weakness Builds the Soul

James Hillman, who is perhaps America's most fertile thinker, suggests that it is our inferiorities that build up our souls. His view is that it is not our strengths that give us depth and character, but our weaknesses. More of us are rendered superficial by our successes than by our failures; more of us are torn apart by our strengths than by our weaknesses.

Reflecting on this, I recall a time some years back when I was a young student studying psychology. One evening I attended a lecture by the renowned Polish psychologist Kazimierz Dabrowski on a concept he called "positive disintegration". His theory was that we grow by first falling apart. At one point, I raised this objection: "Can't we also grow by being built up by our successes, by taking in positive affirmation and letting it purify us of our selfishness?" His answer supports Hillman: "Theoretically, yes, we can grow through our successes, just as easily as we can through our failures. But I can say this, through more than 40 years of psychiatric practice I have rarely seen it. Almost always deep growth takes place through the opposite – our death, our losses, our dark nights of the soul."

It is not that these are, in and of themselves, good; it is just that when we listen to them we grow deep. They build up our souls. Inferiorities and failures are not things to be buried as private and past shames. They are to be listened to. They are entries into the depth of our souls.

Inferiorities and failures are entries into the depth of our souls.

Thinking Small

I have always found it ironic that we easily forget the big things, the events that seem of great importance: Who won the Academy Awards five years ago? Who won the Cup Final? We quickly tend to forget these things. What we do not forget, with all the healing and grace it brought, is who was nice to us all those years ago on the playground at school. Conversely, we also remember, and remember vividly, with all the scars it brought, who laughed at us on the playground and who made fun of our clothes or called us stupid.

Small acts, of cruelty or kindness, leave their effect long after the events have passed. There is, I believe, a profound lesson in this. The kingdom of God, as Jesus tells us, is about mustard seeds, about small seemingly unimportant things, but which, in the long run, are the big things.

Not much in our world today helps us to believe that. Almost everything urges us to think big and to be careless about small things played out on the smaller stage of our personal lives – in our families, marriages, and in our exchanges with our neighbours and colleagues. The little insults that we hand out, the small infidelities within our sexual lives, the many little acts of selfishness – these are deemed to be of little consequence. And, conversely, our small acts of sacrifice and selflessness, the little compliments that we hand out, these are not valued much in our culture. But in the end, the only thing we may remember from a given year is some small mustard seed of cruelty or kindness.

Small acts, of cruelty or kindness, leave their effect long after the events have passed.

A Transparent Life

"You are as sick as your sickest secret!" That's an axiom popular among people in 12-step programmes. They know that until one faces oneself, in searing honesty, before another human being and there acknowledges openly his or her sins, there will always be addictions, rationalisation, and lack of transparency. This is a pivotal and non-negotiable step in every 12-step programme. Without it, at a certain point, all real growth stops.

The Church has always had its own version of this step. We call it confession, the sacrament of reconciliation. Fewer people are going to confession these days. This is an unfortunate development because private confession is one of the pillars of the spiritual life. At a certain point in one's growth, there is no progress without it. The critics of the sacrament of reconciliation are right in saying that God is not tied to one vehicle as an avenue for the forgiveness of sins. They are wrong, however, when they denigrate the importance of a good private confession.

Simply put, confession is the sacrament of the mature and one grows mature by confessing one's sins. One may not need to confess one's sins explicitly to another human being in order to have them forgiven. But one does have to confess them explicitly if he or she hopes to live a transparent life, free of dark skeletons in the closet, and to make progress in the spiritual life.

Private confession is one of the pillars of the spiritual life.

The Agony in the Garden

We tend to misunderstand "the passion of Jesus". Spontaneously we think of it as the pain of the physical sufferings he endured on the road to his death. Partly that misses the point. Jesus' passion should be understood as *passio*, passivity, a certain submissive helplessness he had to undergo in counter-distinction to his power and activity. His passion begins in the Garden of Gethsemane, immediately after he has celebrated the Last Supper. The Scriptures tell us that he went out into the garden with his disciples to pray for the strength he needed to face the ordeal that was now imminent.

It's significant that this agony takes place in a garden. In archetypal literature (and Scripture, among other things, is this kind of literature), a garden is not a place to pick cucumbers and onions. It is the place of delight, the place of love, the place to drink wine, the place where lovers meet in the moonlight, the place of intimacy. It's Jesus, the lover, the one who calls us to intimacy and delight with him, who sweats blood in the garden.

Jesus' agony is that of the lover who's been misunderstood and rejected in a way that is mortal and humiliating. It's his entry into the darkest black hole of human existence, the black hole of bitter rejection, aloneness, humiliation, and helplessness.

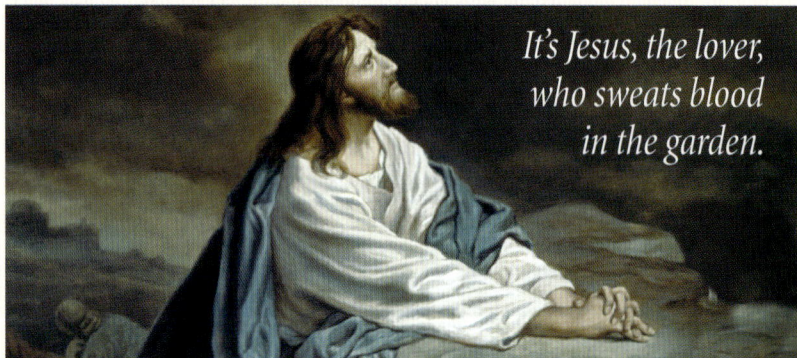

It's Jesus, the lover, who sweats blood in the garden.

GOODSALT

A Place to Sweat Blood

In describing Jesus in the Garden of Gethsemane, Luke says this: "In his anguish he prayed even more earnestly, and his sweat fell to the ground like great drops of blood."

Some years ago, there was a TV series entitled *Thirtysomething*. One episode went this way: A group of married men gathered for a social evening at a hotel. One of the men found himself attracted to the hotel manager with whom he had to deal all evening in terms of arranging food, music, and drink. She was attracted to him, too, and the romantic chemistry intensified. Finally, the moment came to part. The man stalled, thanking her again for her help. She, not wanting to lose the moment, asked him, "Would you like to get together again sometime?" The man hesitated, guiltily apologised for not being more forthright earlier, and did what few have the moral courage to do. Not without sweating a little blood, he said: "I'm married. I need to go home to my wife."

My dad, perhaps the most moral man I've ever known, used to say: "Unless you can sweat blood, you'll never keep a commitment, in marriage, in priesthood, or anywhere. That's what it takes!" He was right. One of the great lessons of Gethsemane is precisely that. To keep any commitment, we have to sweat blood because, like Jesus in the garden, there comes a time when we have to enter into a great loneliness, the loneliness of fidelity and of responding to a higher will and a higher eros. The lover in Jesus had to let go of some things. The same is true for each of us.

To keep any commitment,
we have to sweat blood.

Beware the Sleep of Sorrow

As Jesus and his disciples enter the Garden of Gethsemane, he tells them: "Stay awake, watch!" The implication is that they're about to learn something, a lesson is to be taught. But, as we know, they fell asleep, not because the hour was late and they were tired, nor even because of the wine they'd drunk at the supper. They fell asleep, Luke says, "out of sheer sorrow". They fell asleep because they were disappointed, confused, depressed.

This is one of the perennial temptations we have in life, to fall asleep out of sorrow. Most times when we give in to weakness or commit sin we do so not out of malice or bad intent, but out of despair. Why are we sometimes so petty? Why are we sometimes less than the gracious, understanding, and forgiving persons we would like to be? Simply put, some deep disappointment has rendered us asleep to what's highest inside of our own selves. Depression has rendered us powerless to our own goodness.

It's not easy to stay awake to the lesson Jesus was trying to teach in the Garden of Gethsemane. Because of sleep, the disciples missed the lesson they were supposed to learn from watching Jesus in his prayer. What was that lesson? They were supposed to see and grasp the intrinsic connection between suffering and transformation, and the necessity, in that process, of being willing to carry tension and disappointment without giving in to despair.

***

"Stay awake, watch!"

Preparing for the Contest

In the Gethsemane accounts we're told that, right after being strengthened by an angel, Jesus gets up off the ground and walks with courage to face the ordeal that awaits him. His agony and the strengthening he receives within it readied him for the pain that lay ahead. Indeed, at the time of Jesus, the word agony had a double sense. Beyond its more obvious meaning, it also referred to a particular readying that an athlete would do just before entering the arena or stadium. An athlete would work up a certain sweat (*agonia*) with the idea that this exercise and the lather it produced would concentrate and ready both his energies and muscles for the contest.

The gospel writers want us to have this same image of Jesus as he leaves the Garden of Gethsemane. His agony has brought about a certain emotional, physical, and spiritual lather so that he is now readied, a focused athlete, properly prepared to enter the battle. Moreover, because his strengthening brings a certain divine energy, he is indeed more ready than any athlete.

Good Fridays await us all. We must work up the spiritual lather that readies our souls and bodies for the contest that lies ahead.

Good Fridays await us all.

Moving Toward Courage

We have nothing to fear but fear itself; easily said, but mostly our lives are dominated by it. We may be sincere and good, but we're also fearful. Fearful of pain, of losing loved ones, of misunderstanding, of sickness, of opposition, and ultimately of death. Deep inside us is a powerful pressure to do whatever it takes to ensure our own lives, safety, and security.

And so it's not on the basis of nature that we give our lives away or move towards real courage. We cannot walk from self-pampering to self-sacrifice, from living in fear to acting in courage, and from cringing before the unknown to taking the leap of faith, without first, like Jesus in Gethsemane, readying ourselves through a certain *agonia*, that is, without undergoing the painful sweat that comes from facing what will be asked of us if we continue to live the truth. When Pilate threatens Jesus with death, Jesus stands in freedom and courage because he had already given his life over freely the night before. He is ready for whatever awaits him.

Choosing self-preservation is not necessarily choosing life. Sometimes we need to accept opposition to choose community; sometimes we need to accept bitter pain to choose health; sometimes we need to accept a fearful free-fall to choose safety; and sometimes we need to accept death in order to choose life. If we let fear stop us from doing that, our lives will never be whole again.

---

*Sometimes we need to accept death
in order to choose life.*

Prayer in Dark Times

In the Garden of Gethsemane, as he sweated the blood of loneliness and misunderstanding, Jesus dropped to his knees in prayer. From Jesus' prayer in the garden, we can learn how we too should pray in a dark time. Five elements might be highlighted:

1. *Childlike intimacy with and reliance upon God.* Jesus begins his prayer with the words, "*Abba*, Father". *Abba* is a word that, at the time, a child would use affectionately for his or her father, roughly equivalent to our words "Daddy" or "Papa".

2. *Trust in God, despite overpowering darkness and chaos.* "All things are possible for you." Jesus prays in trust, not just when truth seems to be prevailing, but also, and especially, when falsehood seems to be triumphing.

3. *Radical honesty and boldness in expressing fear.* "Let this cup pass." Jesus tells God where he's really at, frightened and reluctant before bitter duty. There's no denial or pretence in his prayer. Iris Murdoch once wrote: "A common soldier dies without fear. Jesus died afraid."

4. *The willingness to give God the space within which to be God.* "Yet not my will, but yours be done." Despite everything in him that cringes before the implications of saying yes, Jesus gives God the space to fulfil his purposes.

5. *Repetition, repeated prayer.* "He returned and prayed even more earnestly." Scripture promises that faith and prayer will move mountains, but it doesn't promise that they will move them immediately. Sometimes, for prayer to be effective, it has to be prayed many times.

From Jesus' prayer in the garden, we can learn how we too should pray in the dark time.

The Lamb of God

Jesus is the lamb who takes away the sins of the world. That's the central piece in the Christian notion of salvation. It has a variety of expressions, but always the same meaning: Jesus' suffering takes away our sins. Scripture expresses this in metaphors and we must be careful, precisely, to not turn metaphor into literal understanding here. God didn't need to see Jesus suffer horrific pain and humiliation in order to forgive us for sin. God doesn't have to be appeased; though, granted, that's what the metaphor "lamb of God" can suggest. Jesus took away sin by absorbing and transforming sin. How?

Perhaps an image might be helpful: Jesus took away our sins in the same way a filter purifies water. A filter takes in impure water, holds the impurities inside of itself, and gives back only the pure water. It transforms rather than transmits. We see this in Jesus. Like the ultimate cleansing filter he purifies life itself. He takes in hatred, holds it, transforms it, and gives back love; he takes in chaos, holds it, transforms it, and gives back order; he takes in fear, holds it, transforms it, and gives back freedom; he takes in jealousy, holds it, transforms it, and gives back affirmation; he takes in Satan and murder, holds them, transforms them, and gives back only God and forgiveness.

And, in doing this, Jesus doesn't want admirers, but followers. The Garden of Gethsemane invites us, every one of us, to step in, and to step up. It invites us to sweat a lover's blood so as to help absorb, purify, and transform tension and sin rather than simply transmit them.

Jesus took away our sins
in the same way
a filter purifies water.

Our Ignorance of God's Love

"Forgive them, Father, for they know not what they do!" Jesus said this of his executioners. But is it true? A lot indicates that they were far from innocent. How could Jesus' executioners not know what they were doing?

The people who crucified Jesus didn't know what they were doing because they didn't know how much they were loved. That is the blindness and the real ignorance of the executioners. Far too often we crucify others and ourselves because of ignorance, because we feel unloved. For this reason we are harsh in our judgments of others and unaware of why we ourselves are prone to weakness and to compromise our dignity. We are judgmental and weak because, at the end of the day, we don't know any better.

There is a place inside us where each and every one of us is being touched and held unconditionally in love by God.

GOODSALT

43

The type of ignorance that allowed sincere people to crucify Jesus can also explain why so many good, sincere people today are massively blind, communally and individually, to the economic and social demands made by our faith. The real reason we can live so comfortably as the gap between the rich and the poor widens is because we don't know how much we are loved by God, not because we are bad and without conscience. We feel unloved and so we feel we have to take life for ourselves.

Small wonder we settle for second-best or for almost anything else that promises to fill an aching void inside us. Jesus, no doubt, is looking at us and saying: "Forgive them, Father, for they know not what they do!" Too few of us, at any personal level, have ever heard God say to us: "I love you!" Too few of us have ever felt what Jesus must have felt when, at his baptism, he heard his Father say: "You are my beloved child, in you I take delight!" Indeed, most of us have never heard another human being saying this to us, let alone God.

There is a place inside us, a place we are rarely aware of, where each and every one of us is being touched and held unconditionally in love by God. Jesus' executioners acted in a darkness that came from never having had that experience.

The Christ Who Knocks

When I was a young boy, my mother gave me a holy card, an adaptation of a famous painting by Holman Hunt, *Light of the World*. In the version my mother gave me, we see behind a locked door, a man huddled and paralysed by a fear and darkness of some kind. Outside the door stands Jesus, with a lantern, knocking, ready to relieve the man of his burden. But there's a hitch. The door only has a knob on the inside. Jesus cannot enter unless the man first unlocks the door. There's the implication that God cannot help unless we first let God in. Fair enough? Not exactly.

What the cross of Christ reveals is that when we are so paralysed by fear and overcome by darkness that we can no longer help ourselves, when we have reached the stage where we can no longer open the door to let light and life in, God can still come through our locked doors, stand inside our fear and paralysis, and breathe out peace.

God can still come through our locked doors.

The love that is revealed in Jesus' suffering and death, a love that is so other-centred that it can fully forgive and embrace its executioners, can melt frozen hearts, penetrate the walls of fear, descend into our private hells and, there, breathe out peace.

The cross of Christ does not stand helpless before a locked door.

God's Kind of Power

The gospels tell us that when people witnessed Jesus' life and ministry, they saw something that sharply differentiated him from others. "He spoke with great power, unlike the scribes and Pharisees." However, they use a curious word to name that power. They never say that Jesus spoke with great *energia* ("Wow, is he energetic!") or *dynamis* ("What dynamism!"). Instead they use the Greek word *exousia*, a word with no English equivalent, but whose meaning can be conveyed in an image.

If you would put the strongest man in the world in a room with a newborn baby, which of these two beings would be more powerful? Obviously, on one level, the man is more powerful: he could kill the baby if he wanted. But the baby possesses a different kind of power, one that can move things muscles can't. A baby has *exousia:* its vulnerability is a great power. It doesn't need to out-muscle anyone. A baby invites, beckons, and all that's moral and deep in the conscience simply cannot walk away.

It's no accident God chose to be incarnated into this world as a baby. God's power is the power of *exousia*, a baby that lies helpless, muted, patient, beckoning for someone to take care of it. It's this power that lies at the deepest base of things and will, in the end, gently have the final say. It's a power that invites us in.

A baby has exousia: *its vulnerability is a great power.*

PHOTODISC

The Least Important Ones

Six years ago, in Canada's prairies, not far from where I was born and raised, a man named Robert Latimer killed Tracy, his severely-handicapped daughter. He put her into the family truck, hooked a tube to the exhaust-emission, sealed the windows and doors and let her fall asleep. In his mind, this was an act of mercy. He said he loved his daughter and couldn't bear to see her suffer any longer. Her death ignited a national moral and religious debate that has bitterly divided families and communities.

What's the value of a human life such as Tracy Latimer's? Biblically, the answer is clear: When someone is deemed expendable – for whatever reason – at that moment, she or he becomes the most spiritually important person in the community. In the Jewish Scriptures, the prophets emphasise the idea that God has special sympathy for orphans, widows, and strangers. The prophets' message was revolutionary: God has a special sympathy for those whom society deems least important, and how we treat those persons is the litmus test of our faith, morals, and religiosity.

Jesus takes this teaching a notch further, saying: "Whatsoever you do to the least of these, you do to me." Jesus identifies God's presence with the outcasts, with the excluded ones. And he tells us that we have a privileged experience of God in our contact with them. The Tracy Latimers in our lives are in a privileged place where the rest of us can experience God.

God has a special sympathy for those whom society deems least important.

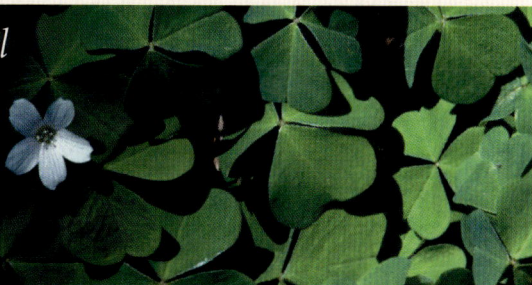

CORBIS

47

Nourished for Service

The Eucharist is not a private act of devotion meant to square our debts with God, but a call to and a grace for service.

The Eucharist is meant to send us out into the world ready to give expression to Christ's hospitality, humility, and self-effacement. Where do we get such a notion? It lies at the very heart of the Eucharist itself. Jesus tells us this when he gives us the Eucharist with the words: "Receive, give thanks, break, and share."

This is everywhere evident in the gospels, though John's Gospel puts it the most clearly. Where the other gospels have Jesus speaking the words of institution at the Last Supper ("This is my body. This is my blood. Do this in memory of me"), John has Jesus washing the disciples' feet. For John, this gesture replaces the words of institution. It specifies what the Eucharist is in fact meant to do, namely, to lead us out of the Church and into the humble service of others.

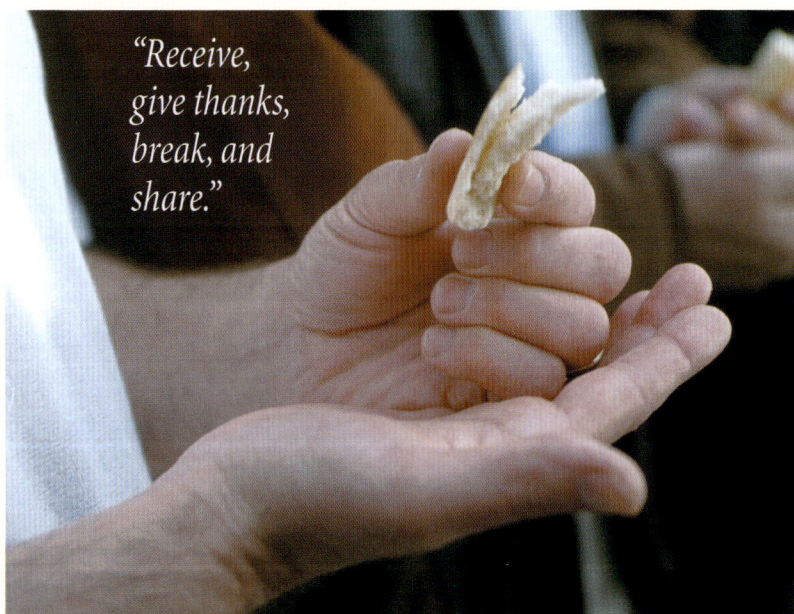

"Receive, give thanks, break, and share."

W.P. WITTMAN

An old hymn, often used to send people forth from church, puts it well:

Called from worship into service
Forth in his great name we go
To the child, the youth, the aged
Love in living deeds to show.

This wonderfully expresses what the Eucharist is meant to do. It is a call to move from worship to service, to take the nourishment, the embrace, the kiss, we have just received from God and the community and translate it immediately and directly into loving service of others. We should be on our knees washing each other's feet because that is precisely what Jesus did at the first Eucharist.

TRIDUUM

How God Feels in This World

H ave you ever been overpowered physically and been powerless to defend yourself or fight back? …then you have felt how God feels in this world.

Have you ever dreamed a dream and found that every effort you made was hopeless and that your dream could never be realised? Have you ever cried tears of shame at your own inadequacy? …then you have felt how God feels in this world.

*God's power in this world
is never the power
of force, of speed,
of physical attractiveness,
or of brilliance.*

Have you ever been shamed in your enthusiasm and not given a chance to explain yourself? Have you ever been misunderstood and powerless to make others see things in your way? …then you have felt how God feels in this world.

Have you ever loved someone and wanted desperately to somehow make him or her notice you and found yourself hopelessly unable to do so? …then you have felt how God feels in this world.

Have you ever felt the world slipping away from you as you grow older and ever more marginalised? …then you have felt how God feels in this world.

Have you ever felt like a minority of one before the group hysteria of a crowd gone mad? If you have ever felt, first-hand, the sick evil of a gang rape, then you have felt how God feels in this world… and how Jesus felt on Good Friday.

God never overpowers. God's power in this world is never the power of force, of speed, of physical attractiveness, or of brilliance. The world's power tries to work that way. But God's power is more muted, more helpless, more shamed, and more marginalised. It lies at a deeper level, at the ultimate base of things, and it will, in the end, gently have the final say.

Waiting for the Resurrection

W e live in difficult times. We've only to watch the news on any given evening. If there's an all-knowing, all-powerful, and all-loving God who is Lord of this universe, his presence isn't very evident on the evening news. There's violence all over the planet, fuelled on every side by self-righteous ideologies

*God lets the universe
right itself the way
a body does when it is
attacked by a virus.*

TRIDUUM

that sanction hatred, by self-interest that lets community fend for itself, and by a socially-approved greed that lets the poor fend for themselves. It's fair and reflective to wonder: Where is the Resurrection in all of this?

Why is God seemingly so inactive? Where is the vindication of Easter Sunday?

These are important questions, even if they aren't particularly deep or new. They were the questions used to taunt Jesus on the cross: *"If you're the Son of God, come down off that cross! If you're God, prove it! Act now!"* For centuries they prayed for a messiah, a superman, to come and display a power and a glory that would simply overpower evil, but what they got was a helpless baby lying in the straw. And when that baby grew up they wanted him to overthrow the Roman empire, but instead he let himself be crucified.

What the Resurrection teaches is that God doesn't forcibly intervene to stop pain and death. Instead he redeems the pain and vindicates the death. The resurrection of Jesus reveals that there's a deep moral structure to the universe, that the contours of the universe are love and goodness and truth. This structure, anchored at its centre by ultimate love and power, is non-negotiable: You live life its way or it simply won't come out right.

More importantly, the reverse is also true: If you respect the structure and live life its way, what's good and true and loving will eventually triumph, despite everything, like a giant moral immune system that brings the body back to health. God lets the universe right itself the way a body does when it is attacked by a virus. We don't have to escape pain and death to achieve victory, we've only to remain faithful, good, and true inside of them. God's day will come.

TRIDUUM

Resurrection Power

The Resurrection is not just something that happened to Jesus 2,000 years ago and will happen to each of us sometime in the future after we die when our own bodies will be raised to new life. It is that, but it is much more.

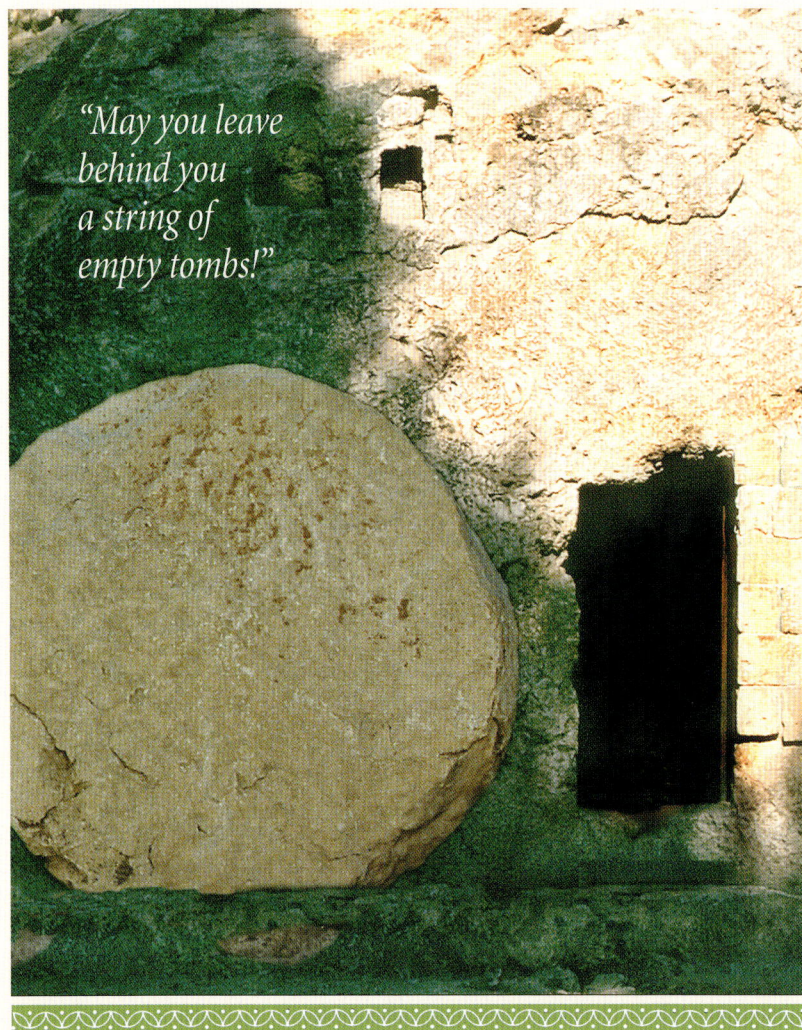

"May you leave behind you a string of empty tombs!"

GENE PLAISTED, OSC

The Resurrection is something that buoys up every moment of life and every aspect of reality. God is always making new life and undergirding it with a goodness, graciousness, mercy, and love that, in the end, heals all wounds, forgives all sins and brings deadness of all kinds to new life.

We feel this resurrecting power in the most ordinary moments of our lives. A sense of the Resurrection, understood in its deepest sense, manifests itself unconsciously in our vitality, in what we call health; in the feeling, however dimly it is sensed, that it is good to be alive. The very atomic structure of the cosmos feels and knows that resurrecting power. That is why it (like us, when we are healthy) pushes forward blindly, buoyed up by a hope that it cannot understand.

A friend of mine once sent me an Easter card that ended with the challenge: "May you leave behind you a string of empty tombs!" That is both my Easter wish and my Easter challenge for all of us. Let our wounded, muted voices begin to sing again: Christ is risen! Life is very, very good! Happy Easter!

Mary of Magdala's Easter Prayer

I never suspected
Resurrection
and to be so painful
to leave me weeping
With Joy
to have met you, alive and smiling, outside an empty tomb
With regret
not because I've lost you
but because I've lost you in how I had you –
in understandable, touchable, kissable, clingable flesh
not as fully Lord, but as graspably human.

I want to cling, despite your protest
cling to your body
cling to your, and my, clingable humanity
cling to what we had, our past.

But I know that… if I cling
you cannot ascend and
I will be left clinging to your former self
…unable to receive your present spirit.

Forgiveness Is the Message

The resurrection of Jesus has many dimensions. At one level, it was a physical event. The dead body of Jesus was raised, the cosmic universe at its deepest level suddenly had a new set of laws, and the very atoms of this universe were rearranged. Something radically new, physically new, as radical and new as the original creation, appeared within history. This aspect should never be understated.

However, the Resurrection was also a spiritual event and that too is important. In the resurrection of Jesus we are given not just the potential for a resurrected body and a resurrected cosmos, we are given as well the possibility of forgiveness, of being forgiven and of forgiving each other. That new possibility and its radical novelty should also never be understated. From the beginning of time until Jesus' resurrection, dead bodies stayed dead. And from Adam and Eve until that same resurrection, wounded and dead hearts stayed wounded and dead. All that has now changed. There are new possibilities.

What is new in the Resurrection is not just the unbelievable new possibility of physical resurrection. The Resurrection gives to us the equally unbelievable possibility of the newness of life that forgiving and being forgiven brings. In our day-to-day lives that is how we are asked to appropriate the Resurrection of Jesus, by forgiving and by letting ourselves be forgiven.

The Resurrection gives us the equally unbelievable possibility of the newness of life that forgiving and being forgiven brings.

The First Creed

The earliest Christians used to have only a single line to their creed: "Jesus is Lord." For them, that said enough. It said everything. It said that at the centre of all things there is a gracious, personal God, and that this God is powerful enough and loving enough to underwrite everything. Jesus believed this. In the Garden of Gethsemane, when everything was crumpling into chaos and darkness and his whole life and message seemed a lie, he prayed: "Father, all things are possible for you."

We believe in the resurrection of Christ, precisely, to the degree that we believe we can, in any circumstance of life, say, and mean, "Lord, all things are possible for you." In the end, this is not a theoretical thing. Faith in the resurrection of Jesus is a practical thing, an everyday trust and sense that there is a deep anchor that is holding everything together. We, for our part, can get on with the business of living, knowing that our inadequacies, failings, and even our deaths, are not the final answer. Faith in the Resurrection is a lived sense that God is still in charge.

"Lord, all things are possible for you." To be able to say that, especially when everything seems to be in contradiction to it, is to truly pray the creed.

*Faith in the Resurrection is a lived sense
that God is still in charge.*

The Rainbow and the Cross

In the Hebrew Scriptures we are presented with the rainbow as a sign of the Resurrection and of God's unconditional love for us. What a beautiful, wonderful, apt symbol! A rainbow bends light so as to refract it and show what it looks like on the inside, its colours, its mystery, its spectacular beauty. Light has a beautiful inside that we can't always see. Scripture tells us that God is light, and in the refraction of light we get to see a little bit of what God looks like on the inside.

The beauty of God is refracted and seen in the moral realm, too. The gospels, for example, tell us that at the precise moment that Jesus died on the cross, "the veil in the Temple was torn from top to bottom". The veil that separated the people from the inner sanctuary was stripped away, allowing them to get a clear view of the holy of holies. Looking at Jesus' death on the cross, we get a clear look into the inside of the holy of holies, namely, an unobstructed look into the inside of God.

Thus the cross does what a rainbow does, only in a different sphere. In a rainbow, we see beneath the surface and we see the spectacular colours that make up light. In the cross, we also see beneath the surface and see the spectacular love, forgiveness, empathy, and selflessness that make up the inside of the moral realm. The rainbow and the cross should never be separated. The beauty of divinity, God's light and God's love, shine through both.

In a rainbow, we see beneath the surface
and we see the spectacular colours
that make up light.

"Come and Have Breakfast!"

Real despair, like all bad demons, is infinitely subtle. What is it? It's the belief that nothing new can ever happen to us. We despair when, however unconsciously, we say: "That is the way I am, that is the way things will always be for me. For me, it is too late." Sadly that prophecy will be self-fulfilling for it is always our desire to be defeated that, in the end, defeats us.

When Jesus was crucified, the first disciples went back to their old way of life, fishing and the sea. They gave up on their dream and went back to their old securities. Then, as John describes, one morning, after a particularly empty night, they smelled fresh fish across the water. A man was bent over a fire, roasting fish. He called to them: "Come and have breakfast!" Nobody had to ask who he was. They knew. God was back.

That incident perfectly describes our own faith struggle. We meet Christ and, for a while, it all seems so real. Then he seems to disappear, to die in our lives, and, in our despair, we go back to fishing and the sea… sitcoms, gossip, routine! Then, when we have long given up, right after a particularly empty night, we smell something fresh coming out of nowhere – and we don't have to ask who or what it is. We know. God is back.

To rule out the possibility of surprise, novelty, absolute newness, is to block the Resurrection. God will come. Our job is to remain open, to be alert for the smell of fresh fish.

We know. God is back.

Stay on the Road to Emmaus

Every generation of Christians must fight its own demons, struggle with its own sadness. Today, in terms of feelings, we live in that particular sadness between Good Friday and Easter Sunday. We are walking on the road to Emmaus. The God, the Church, and the dreams we had as children have died and we are trying to console each other for our crucified dreams.

Yet the old words, the old creeds, the ancient alleluias, still burn holes in us and when we hear the words of Jesus, as we gather for Eucharist, it is still easy enough to sing: "Are not our hearts burning within us?"

We need to remain on the road to Emmaus. The resurrected Christ is there to be met. In his company we need to spill out our sadness, mourn our disappointments, and stir our old hopes. At some moment our eyes will open and we will recognise the crucified Lord in the Risen Christ who is actually walking with us now. Our dreams will explode anew, like a flower bursting into bloom after a long winter, and we will fill with a new innocence as Easter Sunday happens again.

"Are not our hearts
burning within us?"

Daily Resurrections

What the resurrection of Jesus promises is that things can always be new again. It's never too late to start over. Nothing is irrevocable. No betrayal is final. No sin is unforgivable. Every form of death can be overcome. There isn't any loss that can't be redeemed. Every day is virgin.

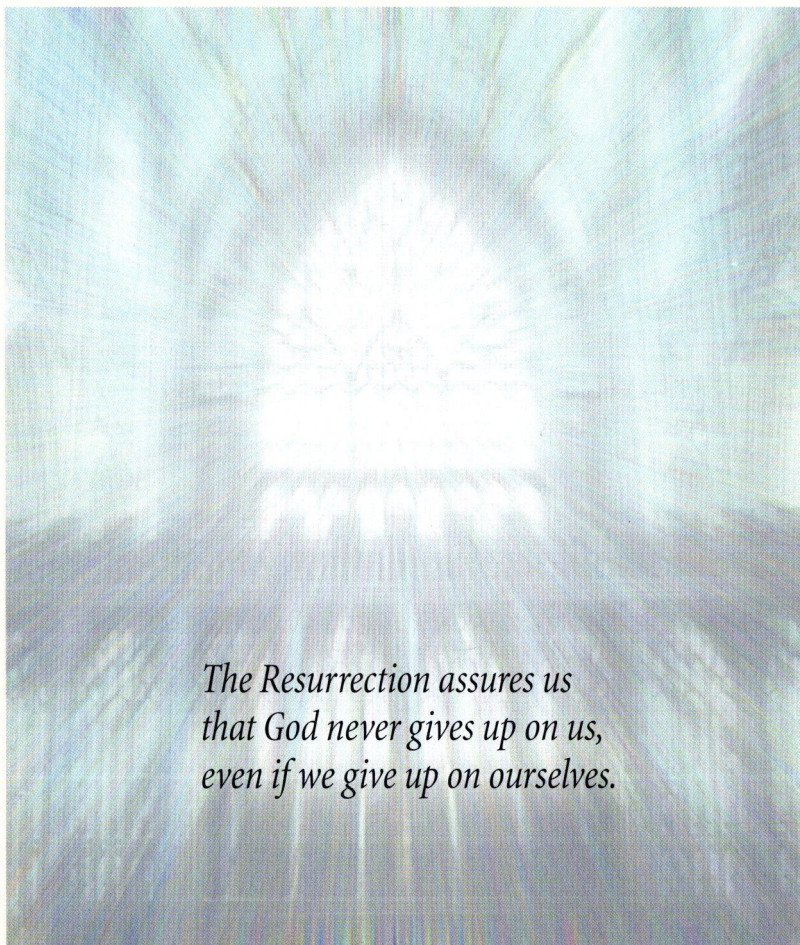

*The Resurrection assures us
that God never gives up on us,
even if we give up on ourselves.*

GOODSALT